D0014331

# Dog Treats

**58** ways
to make your best
friend **happy**

Ray Strobel

sourcebooks

Copyright © 2011 by Ray Strobel
Cover and internal design © 2011 by Sourcebooks, Inc.
Cover design by Krista Joy Johnson/Sourcebooks
Cover images © Soubrette/iStockphoto
Sourcebooks and the colophon are registered trademarks of Sourcebooks, Inc.

All rights reserved. No part of this book may be reproduced in any form or by any electronic or mechanical means including information storage and retrieval systems—except in the case of brief quotations embodied in critical articles or reviews—without permission in writing from its publisher, Sourcebooks, Inc.

All brand names and product names used in this book are trademarks, registered trademarks, or trade names of their respective holders. Sourcebooks, Inc., is not associated with any product or vendor in this book.

Published by Sourcebooks, Inc.
P.O. Box 4410, Naperville, Illinois 60567-4410
(630) 961-3900
Fax: (630) 961-2168
www.sourcebooks.com

Printed and bound in China.
LEO 10 9 8 7 6 5 4 3 2 1

## Photo Credits

Internal photos © Yuri Arcrs/iStockphoto, p. 19; Tamara Bauer/iStockphoto, p. 21; Caziopeia/iStockphoto, p. 30; Claudia Dewald/iStockphoto, p. 54; Teresa Guerrero/iStockphoto, p. 59; Adam Hester/iStockphoto, p. 49; Emmanuel Hidalgo/iStockphoto, p. 25; Eric Isselée/iStockphoto, p. 33; Offir Kilion/iStockphoto, p. 41; Mark Kolbe/iStockphoto, p. 22; Holly Leitner, pp. 36, 39, 46, 53, 60, 64; Ljupco/iStockphoto, p. 9; Gary Martin/iStockphoto, p. 14; Richard McGuirk/iStockphoto, p. 7; Kati Molin/iStockphoto, p. 45; Lobke Peers/iStockphoto, p. 10; Monique Rodriguez/iStockphoto, p. 29; Paul Roux/iStockphoto, p. 63; Rodolfo Sadeugra/iStockphoto, p. 17; Soubrette/iStockphoto, p. 27; R. G. Strobel, p. 13; Jan Tyler/iStockphoto, p. 35; Martin Valigursky/iStockphoto, p. 57; Birute Vijeikiene/iStockphoto, p. 42; Walik/iStockphoto, p. 51

# Acknowledgments

Thanks to my many friends who volunteered themselves and their canine companions for photography, including Angie, Cathy, Danielle, Emily, Jamie, and Sarah. Special thanks to Sally for her many good suggestions.

Thanks also to my two best friends, Brody and Dewey, for helping me research this book. They let me know with a wag of their tails whenever I discovered something new that makes them happy.

And, of course, thanks to my wife, JoBelle, for searching shelters and rescue organizations and always finding the perfect dogs for us.

# Introduction

When our best friend Bear died after eleven years with us, my wife, JoBelle, beat herself up for months because we never fulfilled our promise to take him to see the ocean.

"We told him so many times we would take him," she said. "He would have loved to run in the surf. But we never seemed to find the time."

I, on the other hand, berated myself for not taking him to Paris—although that promise was more to make me happy than him. When I was in France, I missed Bear as I watched other dog lovers enjoy having their companions right by their sides in cheese shops, restaurants, boutiques, cafés, and wine bars. I wanted him to be there with me.

Looking back, I think we treated Bear lovingly for all those years, but I still have nagging doubts whenever I see people enjoying an event or activity with their dogs that he and I never shared. When I visit his grave in our yard, I find myself apologizing for not doing more with him. I have come to realize, though, as I look back on the wonderful times we shared together, that it's not about regrets but about memories—good memories.

And that's what I hope you'll discover on the following pages: things to do with or for your best friend to make him or her happy, and things that will create lasting memories for you.

# 1 take your dog on a long fall walk through crunching leaves

Choose a crisp, sun-filled fall day, take your dog on a walk through the fallen leaves, and reflect on nature's beauty. Walk slowly; it's better if you linger.

It's a wonderfully relaxing way to spend time with your friend. Do it now, and in years to come, whenever a leaf crunches beneath your feet, you'll smile with fond remembrance.

# 2 lay on a blanket together and gaze at the stars

Your dog is probably not used to being out with you after dark, so this will be an exciting adventure.

Wait for a crystal clear night. Find a quiet spot for quiet thoughts. Don't bring treats; you'll want your dog to concentrate and meditate, too.

As you gaze upward, you'll find you can't help but experience wonder. The wonder of stars, the wonder of life—the wonder of dogs.

REX

*take your dog on a long fall walk through crunching leaves*

## 3 tell your dog a secret nobody else knows

It doesn't have to be a deep, dark secret. Something light and frivolous will do, as long as no one else knows it. There's something special about being able to whisper, "It's just between the two of us."

You know you can trust *this* friend not to tell. And, even more importantly, not to judge you, either.

## 4 build a snowdog together

Sometimes it's cold outside, and we use that as an excuse not to take our friend out as often as we should. Here's an activity that will make you look forward to the frosty weather: build a snowdog, modeled to look like your favorite furry friend. Build a snowman, too, with a stick for a leash to walk the snowdog.

Your creation might not last long, but there's no need to bring a camera along to record it for posterity. Even though it will melt soon, your memories won't.

ANNIBELLE

*tell your dog a secret nobody else knows*

ROSCO

*take your dog with you on vacation*

## 5 take your dog with you on vacation

There's nothing worse than the "we shouldn't have left Rosco home" feeling.

It doesn't have to be Las Vegas or London or Rome. It's not about the destination; it's about sharing the experience. A weekend at a bed and breakfast in the country or a big city "dogs welcome" hotel would suffice. Before you head to your destination, research dog-friendly accommodations in the area.

Vacations are for relaxing and feeling good, both of which are easier with your best friend at your side.

## 6 pose with your pooch

You see her do it every day: downward-facing dog! Why not join her? A little relaxing will be good for the both of you. Search for doga (dog yoga) classes in your area so your dog can reach the Zen state of mind with you.

Concentrate, meditate. Both of you. It's quality quiet time together.

## 7 drive down a country road with the windows wide open

Expressways don't count, because it's not just about speed. It's about the country sights, sounds, and smells: row upon row of corn, acres of wheat, or cattle roaming in the distance.

As you pick up speed and your dog closes his eyes, it's not because the wind is too much for him. On the contrary, he's just dreaming, "I could run this fast...free and fast...under my own power. I could run down that deer or antelope...I just know I could."

## 8 take a family portrait *every* year

Gather the family together for a special snapshot, dog included. It doesn't have to be an extravagant production, just a simple reminder of good times. If you're feeling fancy, though, dress everyone up in finery—including your furry friend. Take the same photo at the same time each year, to show how you've all grown together.

ROCKY & BEAR

*drive down a country road with the windows wide open*

BELLA

*share a quiet spot*

## 9  share a quiet spot

Find a calm, secluded spot where you can go to laugh, talk softly to one another, and get away from the cacophony of everyday life. A spot you both can call "our place."

Go there often. When all else has passed, this secret place will remain in your heart.

## 10  bistro, table for two

Research your area for restaurants that have outdoor seating and allow dogs. Pull up a seat, relax, and watch your dog enjoy a night out beside you. If you can't find a dog-friendly restaurant, opt for take-out and dine at a nearby park. If you're really adventurous, take your pooch to Paris. The dog-loving City of Light welcomes canines with open arms, outdoors and in.

## 11  push him to his limits

Your parents always demanded that you live up to your potential. Too often, we don't give our dogs the opportunity to do the same.

Learn about your dog's breed (or, more likely, various breeds); discover what he needs for a more fulfilling life. It won't be the same for a pit bull and a pug, a beagle and a boxer. Each breed will have different needs.

This may require sledding with your husky or playing chess with your border collie. Whether your dog requires more swimming or running, fetching or napping, make it a priority to give him his heart's desire.

## 12  personalize your plates

When you're out and about, your car can announce to the world that you're lucky enough to have a dog as your best friend.

If your dog's name is already taken, come up with a creative alternative, like "ILUVMAX," "MYMAGGIE," "MOLLYNME," or—one of my favorites—"RESCUDOG."

LOUIE

*push him to his limits*

## 13 kiss your pooch firmly on the lips

Go for it! Plant a big one, smack dab where it counts, when you want to say, "I love you!"

She'll probably think it's no big deal—no different than any other kiss. But you'll know the difference.

## 14 sneak your dog in...

...to a movie theater, a nice restaurant, a Starbucks. It's fun, it's naughty... but your friend will think it's nice.

They don't make purses big enough to hide Great Danes or greyhounds, but plenty are large enough for toy poodles, pugs, Pomeranians, and the like. Think of how much better *Must Love Dogs* would have been with Molly in your lap sharing your popcorn. Or how much better that steak would have tasted if you had surreptitiously slipped a few bites into your lap for Buster.

SALLY

*kiss your pooch firmly on the lips*

## 15 take your dog cruising on a bike

Bring the small dog in your life along for a big experience.

Whether in the city or country, he'll experience sights, sounds, and smells going by at a faster pace than his little legs would normally carry him.

You'll pedal—he'll enjoy.

## 16 don't take a bad day out on your dog

Here's a promise to make to yourself: don't kick the dog. Sometimes it's easy to release your frustrations on your furry friend, but remember, he's not (usually) the cause of your troubles.

Instead, allow him to do what he's good at—turning your bad days into good nights, just by being quietly at your side.

ARNOLD

*take your dog cruising on a bike*

SAM

*serve your dog an expensive steak*

## 17 serve your dog an expensive steak

Even if your dog doesn't remember it the next day, you'll remember it for years—the look on his face when he first spied that slab of beef. "Is that for me?!"

It's a memory that's guaranteed to always bring a smile to your face, and that's worth a lot more than a few bucks.

## 18 let your dog choose the toy

Take your buddy to your favorite pet store and let him roam the aisles. Let him sniff, test, and nibble on a few possibilities. Then go back through the selection a second time so he's sure. He'll pick out his favorite and proudly carry it to the checkout counter.

You think you know what's best for him, but you might be surprised by what he chooses for himself.

His choice will probably last for less time than the toys you selected for him, but maybe that just means he liked it more.

## 19 watch the sun set together

Search for the perfect spot. It might take a while to discover, but you'll be thankful you found it as you enjoy the beauty and the quiet moments with your very best friend.

And forever after, when others exclaim, "Wow, what a great sunset!," you'll find yourself replying, "Let me tell you about a *really* beautiful one..."

## 20 tap into your friend's thoughts

If you've always wanted to be able to look deeper into your dog's mind and better understand his thoughts, here's an idea. Spend some time researching the science of canine emotions by looking online, reading a book, or talking to an expert about the subject. Get to the heart of how he's feeling and find out how you can help your friend be as happy as possible.

HALLY

*watch the sun set together*

## 21 really rub the tummy

Of course you rub her tummy—a lot—and she loves it. Instead of saying, "There...that's enough for now," see if you have the stamina to keep it up until *she* declares she's had enough. You might be surprised at how long it takes, but you'll be glad you did it (and so will she).

## 22 splurge on a great bed for your dog

*Of course* he sleeps with you at night, but he also spends a lot of time napping during the day, and he needs a quality bed of his own. He'll get almost as much pleasure from lounging in luxury as you'll get from watching him.

FLO

*really rub the tummy*

## 23   question the costume

It's fun to dress up our dogs, especially at Halloween. Just don't get carried away. Here's a good rule of thumb: don't embarrass her.

Your friend shouldn't look any sillier than you do in your costume.

## 24   immortalize his name... in frosting!

Go online, find a dog-friendly cookie recipe, and write his name on the creation to make it even more special.

No, he won't know the difference. You'll give him the cookie, and he'll wolf it down without even noticing that you've written his name in frosting. So it's not for him, it's for you. It's about a fun afternoon together making memories you can put away in your memory bank.

WANDA & MUFFIN

*question the costume*

SUE

*roll in the grass and laugh*

## 25 roll in the grass and laugh

Don't worry about grass stains—it's time for some goofy fun!

Tell a joke, make a funny face, roll her over for teasing and tickling. Roughhouse! Get her laughing (like you will be).

There are all kinds of happy times we share with our friends, but the ones we remember most fondly are often the silliest.

## 26 buy that cheap toy (again)

Remember that cheap stuffed toy you bought? The one your dog destroyed in five minutes?

Maybe it wasn't shoddy construction that resulted in its early demise. Maybe it was something unknown to you that drove your dog into a wonderfully happy, fantastic frenzy that would have destroyed a truck tire.

Buy him the same toy again, and let him relive the frenzy. And don't complain; enjoy those five minutes as much as he likely will.

## 27 let your dog sit on the good furniture

You can always repair or replace furniture, but it's harder to mend your heart. So let your dog play. Let her lounge on your chaise, crash into your Chippendale. So what? What (or who) is more important in the end?

## 28 treat your dog to a day at the spa

So you get her groomed once in a while. That doesn't count. A spa day for you is something special—why not create one for her?

Pedicure, bath, massage, teeth cleaning, deep dethatching, maybe even a color tint to her coat or a punk haircut for a little added fun. The whole nine yards.

If you don't want to venture out, pamper your pet at home. Put her in your tub, give her a blow dry, and toss her some new fluffy pillows. Let her unwind for a few hours.

SASHA

*let your dog sit on the good furniture*

## 29 invite *her* friends to *her* party

Remember, when you throw a party for your best friend, it's *her* party, not yours. Your dog will want a few extra legs on the guests.

And you don't need a birthday or other special occasion to send out the invites. Any day can be a good time to ask her friends over for a play date. Let them sniff and snort, run and play together.

## 30 tell your dog you love him *every* day

Tell him *every* day—whisper it in his ear, shout it when you walk through the door—so you'll never doubt he knows.

PETE, MARVIN, & MAXINE

*invite* her *friends* to her *party*

BRUTUS

i (heart) my pooch

## 31 i (heart) my pooch

Arm, ankle, wrist—get a permanent memory of your dog anywhere you want. If your pooch's name is too "cute" (Princess or Poopsie) or too "butch" (Fang or Tiger) to be in plain sight, you can have it rendered in Chinese, Hebrew, or Cyrillic.

Even before the pain subsides, pull your friend aside, show her your new artwork, and say, "Look, you and me, together—always."

## 32 take your friend to work

June 25th is the official "Take Your Dog to Work Day," but why wait?

It may be tough if you're a heart surgeon or air traffic controller, but maybe, just maybe, you could get away with it if you're a cabbie, a forest ranger—or the boss.

Having your friend by your side is guaranteed to make your day go faster, but, more importantly, it will give him a better understanding of what you do when you leave him alone all day. (When you come home with a bag of groceries, he thinks you've been out hunting.)

## 33 paint your pooch's portrait

Don't worry about the outcome; just close your eyes and create with your heart.

Even if her fur or ears or eyes don't turn out just right, you might be surprised at how you capture your dog's inner beauty.

No matter how many photos you have of the two of you, nothing will be more personal than this. In your creation, you'll see things others cannot, which is why you'll hang this treasure in a place of honor—forever.

## 34 make a donation in your dog's name to a no-kill shelter

Make it easier for other dogs to find that special someone who will love them as much as you love your pet. Locate a nearby no-kill shelter and send a check. On the memo line, write, "Missy asked me to send this."

ZEUS

*paint your pooch's portrait*

## 35 let your dog experience snow

Northern dog lovers know the joy snow brings every year, when their four-legged companions get to rediscover that strange white stuff.

Gentle flakes falling on the tongue, a soft dusting on the coat, the first tentative "what is this stuff" steps, and then the romping begins. It's something to experience, a sight not to be missed, even by dog lovers living in warm climes.

So, load up the car! Visit the family, the in-laws, or just the nearby mountains. Snow is never that far away.

## 36 give your dog her own Facebook page

Admit it; you're worried she'll have more friends than you do! But create a page for her anyway. It's a great place to post all your photos, to announce the latest trick your dog has mastered, or even to get her fixed up with that special "somedog" that might—just might—be "the one."

WARNER

*let your dog experience snow*

CODY

*let your dog win*

## 37 let your dog win

Everyone wants to be a winner. So let him win once in a while—praise him for his strength and tenacity, and tell him how strong he is. *Boost his ego*! Here's your chance to "throw a match" and feel good about it. He'll feel good, and you will too.

## 38 serve dinner on your heirloom china

Just once in a while will do. Tell her to take it slow; serve her meal in three courses. Just like at a three-star restaurant.

After all, special china is supposed to be for special guests, isn't it? And who's more special?

## (39) share your sleep

Your dog loves being close to you almost as much as you love being close to him, and bedtime is special time. When he's gone and you're sleeping alone, you'll be glad you let him share your bed with you.

Dogs just want to be close to you. Don't deny them—or yourself—that simple pleasure.

## (40) give a full body massage

An occasional pat on the head is all well and good, but you know your best friend deserves more. So prepare yourself to spend a good half hour—ankles, toes, armpits, (legpits?), foot pads. Left side, right side, top to bottom. Again and again. Watch her collapse in ecstasy.

DOG-DOG

*share your sleep*

SARAH

*put your dog's picture on a T-shirt*

## 41 put your dog's picture on a T-shirt

If you're tired of wearing everyone else's logos, then create your own! It will be much better than "I'm With Stupid," or wearing that tattered tee from last decade's Bon Jovi concert.

Hanes or Prada, it doesn't matter. It's the photo that counts. Your pooch will be glad you've made her a star. And why stop at T-shirts? Your friend's photo will look great on coffee mugs, stamps, or coasters, too.

## 42 let *your dog* teach *you*

While teaching your friend how to sit or stay, you might want to consider asking her for a bit of guidance on loving unconditionally.

We accept that our dogs love us this way as if it's normal. But if it's so easy, why do we struggle with loving others unconditionally? Perhaps we should give dogs their due credit.

And ask them to teach us, too.

## 43 drift with your dog

Rent a canoe and find a quiet river. Let the lazy current take the two of you along. *Watch him watch.*

You'll enjoy watching him focus on the activity along the banks and the ever-changing scenery, as you go with the flow.

## 44 remember the doggie bag

Let doggie bags live up to their name. Save some of your meal the next time you eat at a restaurant, and take home the leftovers for your friend to enjoy.

DOOBIE

*drift with your dog*

## 45 let your dog love a child

And let a child love your dog. Dogs need love, but they need to show love, too. It's a shame to deny them that perfect combination of puppy and child.

## 46 write a short story about the two of you

Write a short story about a favorite memory you have with your dog. When time has erased the details that made the event so special, your story will bring them back to light.

This is a piece you'll want to hide away, so, like a fine wine, it can age. Save it for a rainy day in your heart. Pull it out in five or six or seven years and relive the experience.

Sit by the fire and fire up your memories.

TINY

*let your dog love a child*

## 47 share breakfast in bed

Breakfast in bed! It's special when someone else serves you, so now it's your turn. Pancakes for you. Bacon for him. It's a fun way to relax and indulge on a Sunday morning.

Even if your friend is the most mixed of mixed breeds, this will be his breakfast of champions!

## 48 include your dog in holiday celebrations

Wrap a Christmas or Hanukkah present for her, hide a basket full of treats for her on Easter, give her a kiss at midnight on New Year's, and, most importantly, take special time on Thanksgiving to be thankful for having such a loving friend.

GRACE

*share breakfast in bed*

FUZZY

*put your sidekick in your sidecar*

## 49 put your side*kick* in your side*car*

*Vrooooom!* Your giant black lab won't fit in a bicycle basket? Here's a great adventure for the *big* dog in your life.

A sidecar provides all the space you need, so strap him in and pop the clutch. It's much more macho than a bicycle—and that's what all "big dogs" want.

## 50 make some bouillon-flavored ice cubes

Low in calories, high in flavor (and fun factor).

Dissolve a chicken or beef bouillon cube or two in a pot of warm water and make a tray of delicious ice cubes for her. This is a refreshing treat that will make every day a little more special.

## 51 let your dog chase (or be chased by) the surf

Oceans, like dogs, are among God's greatest creations. The two should meet at least once.

Freshwater lakes are all well and good, but every dog should have the opportunity to challenge *the surf*! Chase it, run from it, leap over and through it. Smell it.

Water with salt, seaweed, and shells; all kinds of strange new things to sniff and wonder about. Then the surf will come charging in—let the chase begin!

If water isn't your dog's thing, let your friend run on the beach, sniff the salty air, or just lounge with you as you soak up the sun.

## 52 include your dog in your wedding party

Maybe you're already married, but this one's too fun not to mention! When you look at your photo album in years to come, you'll be happier if you made your four-legged friend part of the festivities.

Flower girl, ring bearer, or just at your feet in the official wedding photos, your dog deserves to be part of your special day.

BOFFO

*let your dog chase (or be chased by) the surf*

## (53) take your dog on a picnic

Spread the blanket—spread the joy. Pack a gourmet basket with special treats for you and your dog, even if you're only venturing as far as your own backyard. Strawberries for you, perhaps, and some thinly sliced filet mignon for him.

Don't worry about bugs. Your dog will want to play with the grasshoppers and nudge the ants. You should enjoy nature, too. Bask in the sun, nap together, and enjoy a lazy day.

## (54) let your dog lead

Just for a day, don't tug on his leash or pull him along. Let him lead the way at his own chosen speed, not yours. Let him stop and sniff, if he so desires. Don't get frustrated; you're in no hurry today.

LEWIS

*take your dog on a picnic*

DEWEY

*read the Sunday comics together*

## 55 read the Sunday comics together

Try comic strips featuring a dog, of course: *Peanuts, Get Fuzzy, Mutts*, or *Mr. Boffo* (for his wonder dog, Weederman). Spread the paper on the living room floor, snuggle up next to your friend, and get comfortable. Make it a Sunday ritual.

## 56 name someone (or something) after her

When someone exclaims, "You named your *dog* after your kid?!," you can reply, "No, I named my *kid* after my dog."

Why name your new pooch after someone famous? Name her what you want, then name someone (or something) after *her*. Her name will live on! She'll appreciate the gesture.

## 57 share a cone

Lick, lick. Share yours, or buy him his own baby cone, and just share the experience. In small amounts, ice cream won't hurt him. Let your friend do what you do: enjoy a little bit of something that might not be the best for you...but tastes so good.

Of course, sharing the cone is symbolic—it represents how you want to share all of the good things in life with your friend.

## 58 spread the joy

Why should you get all the joy your companion has to offer? Such joy is too wonderful a feeling to keep all for yourself.

Make arrangements to visit a nursing home, retirement home, or children's hospital, and bring your best friend. See how quickly he makes new friends. Just when you thought your dog couldn't possibly bring you more happiness, you'll discover otherwise.

HANS

*share a cone*

# About the Author

BRODY  DEWEY

Ray Strobel is the author of eight books, including *A Black Eye Isn't the End of the World.* A few years ago, Ray and his wife, JoBelle, lost their two original canine companions, Bear and Rocky, during one long, sad summer. As most dog lovers who suffer the death of a loving companion do, they swore never to adopt another dog, believing others could never fill their hearts the same way.

But their house was too quiet and their hearts too empty, so along came Brody and Dewey. All four dogs were adopted.